MY STORY OF HOW I OVERCAME

I'M STRONGER

PARALYSIS AND

I'M WISER

DEPRESSION

I'M BETTER

BY

JONATHAN COLLINS

Thank You
&
Keep God First

www.mrjaycollins.com
Instagram: Mr_Jay_Collins

Jonathan Collins

Lolana Mack Publishing

©2020
ISBN: 978-0-9977804-6-8
Published by: Lolana Mack Publishing
(lolanamackpublishing@gmail.com)

Layout: Coach Wright Publications

Cover Design: Jonathan Collins

FOREWORD

Watching this strong, handsome and loving young man's body be destroyed by Guillain-Barre syndrome was "Gut Wrenching". To walk in Jonathan's hospital room and see how this terrible disease was destroying his body was more than even I, an experienced nurse, could take. I recognized his face, but I did not recognize the body. The body attached to Jonathan's face was atrophied and resembled an elderly bedridden man. To see this healthy young man having to be fed all his meals and to have to rely on others to meet his simple needs such as holding the telephone was hard to bare. I fought back many tears, especially when I had to leave to go home from visiting him in the hospital.

One day that stands out in my mind, was an evening I stopped by to feed Jonathan his dinner. He was unaware that I had entered his hospital room. The nurses were busy repositioning Jonathan in his bed because he was unable to use his hands or feet to move himself. As I glanced over at his hands and feet, I could see that the muscles had started to waste away. He had the appearance of an elderly bedridden man. At that moment, with tears in my eyes, I realized that he may never walk again. Having been a nurse for several years, I had never seen a patient with such severe muscle wasting walk again. I began to question GOD. How could this have happened to such a healthy young man? He was an avid basketball player, with a strong musculature and zero body fat and a good kid. Jonathan and his sisters had already suffered through the tragic loss of their mother, now Guillain-Barre syndrome. In that moment I began to PRAY silently and ask GOD to restore Jonathan from the" crown of his head to the sole of his feet". As I lifted my head from my silent prayer, Jonathan noticed that I had arrived, and he gave me a huge smile. He has always been known for his huge smile, but I wasn't expecting such a warm greeting. Fighting back the tears, it was then I knew GOD was in control. His smile helped to elevate my faith level in GOD. If he could smile through all that he was going through; with the unknowns of this disease, then surely, I could stand in agreement for his healing.

I have learned these principles from Jonathan's journey: GOD is in control, the power of prayer, and never give up (keep fighting). These principles from his journey also helped me to understand what Psalm 23 truly means:" Though I walk through the valley of the shadow of death I will fear no evil because the Lord is with me"

Jonathan was always pleasant and had kind words for others. He was always concerned with the welfare of others even though he was in a battle for his life. Exceeding the expectation of his doctors, his nurses and therapist admired his strength. Jonathan's journey was not only for his growth and development in GOD, it was also for others to see GOD and his awesome power. To see him today is to see GOD and his healing power. I truly believe GOD has a greater work for him to do.

I remember visiting Jonathan at the hospital when he was newly diagnosed, and he looked his weakest. He was lying in bed and he couldn't even turn over in bed by himself. He was total care. He looked at me with a smile on his face and said, "You know I am going to walk again". He said these words to me with no hesitation in his voice.

As I watched his drive and momentum to fight against this terrible disease it gave me hope. I watched how he would work through his therapy sessions and go back to his room and workout over and over again. He was so driven, his therapist, nurses and doctors were amazed at his progress. He never grew tired of trying to beat the odds. He became my greatest inspiration.

Kecia Williams

Jonathan Collins

I'm Stronger I'm Wiser I'm Better

Table of Content

I'm Stronger I'm Wiser I'm Better

Chapter 1

A Walk of Faith

"Believing is seeing. You gotta believe
something will happen for you before you see it.
Have faith in the process of getting there"

-Unknown

As the doors closed behind me, I stood motionless at the curb taking in a deep breath of fresh air. I was so grateful for my life and for the ability to be walking without any assistance. Leaving, I was totally different from the young man that had wobbled in over four months earlier with flu like symptoms and pain in my legs, totally unsuspecting of the difficult journey that was ahead for me. As I packed my belongings the night before, I thought back over the past several months and felt a sense of jubilation and gratefulness. I had accumulated lots of things in that one room, as it had been my home for quite some time. Having been so excited about leaving, it was nonetheless a sleepless night. Knowing I would need my rest and strength to accomplish what I had planned, I tried hard to get some sleep. I had been determined to walk out on my own. As the time drew near, I was asked again about my departure. It is customary for those being discharged from the hospital to be taken out in a wheelchair. I had proclaimed quite emphatically that I would be WALKING out of the hospital, and with no assistance.

Finally, the day had come for me to make my exit back into the real world. I felt that I had been on the longest trip I had ever taken in my entire life. The feeling was indescribable, knowing that I had just a few weeks earlier harbored a great deal of fear about leaving the hospital. This was mainly due to the fact that I

14

would be leaving in a wheelchair and I had the added stress and anxiety of how I would fit in, how I would take care of myself and live a normal life. I stood with a great smile on my face as I prepared to leave. I didn't remember that hallway being quite so long. It was definitely a walk to remember. The walk was long, tiring, difficult and yet exhilarating all at the same time. As I made my way down the hall, I stopped to say good-bye to my neighbors and the staff that had not already come by my room to say good-bye, prior to my leaving. My legs were still very weak and even standing in the elevator, as it took me to the ground floor, was difficult. Having said my goodbyes to the place I had known as home for the past couple of months and to the people that had been my help and support as well, I was ready to begin a new chapter in my life. As I stood there on the curb, just outside the hospital doors, I realized I was stronger, wiser and better and ready to face the world and whatever came next!

Chapter 2

The Unexpected

"Health is not valued until sickness comes"

-Thomas Fuller

There I was with a son in 2007, trying to figure out how to be a great single father at a young age, as his mom and I were not together. I had just been introduced to a life of drinking and partying; A life that I knew nothing about previously. Modeling and playing basketball in some different adult basketball leagues were passions that occupied a great deal of my time. My greatest example of a father and family man was my grandfather, who had five children, worked three jobs and was a strong Christian man. He taught me how to work with my hands among other things and I felt that he was on a pedestal that I could never reach as far as being a great father. He was the head of the usher board at church and had groomed me to be a Jr. usher. My sibling and I all grew up in the church and knew the significance of prayer. We had a very close-knit family including two sisters that I grew up with and with whom I had a strong bond.

What I knew to be normal about my life began to change rather quickly around November of 2008. Here I was in what I thought was the prime of my life; young, strong, athletic and in good physical shape. I was employed as a manager in a Retail store and had a great relationship with my girlfriend and was happy. It all began suddenly. I somehow got the flu and was using Theraflu and other hot beverages as a futile attempt to manage my symptoms. I was actually feeling quite miserable but did not allow it to slow me down.

My girlfriend and I went to have Thanksgiving dinner at her family's home. Although I didn't feel well, I didn't pass up the opportunity to partake in the alcoholic beverages being consumed. Joining in, I drank heavily. Making every effort to self-medicate, I continued to go to work and never went to the doctor and then came a severe migraine headache that was unbearable; It hurt to open my eyes, hear sound and the light was piercing which caused me to cover my head in every attempt to block out both sound and light.

On the following Sunday my girlfriend and I went Christmas shopping. While in the store, I began to feel very weak and experience pain in my legs. I was forced to use a shopping cart to balance myself. The pain was quickly accompanied by a tingling in my hands and on the bottom of my feet. At the suggestion of my girlfriend, I googled Web MD and looked up my symptoms. According to Web MD the symptoms could be a result of diabetes. The fact that diabetes ran in my family made what I was reading more credible and I was somewhat comfortable with accepting that diagnosis. We managed to finish our shopping; however, I was unable to make it to the basketball game in which I was scheduled to play that weekend. The intimate moments shared with my girlfriend over the weekend were different and I had the strange and overwhelming feeling that this would be the last time we shared intimacy.

On Monday December 8, 2008, I woke up, looked outside and noticed that it was snowing. Having planned to go over to my grandmother's and wrap my Christmas gifts, I did not allow the snow to deter me. As I proceeded to get dressed and prepare to leave, I noticed that I was feeling very tired and drained. In my mind I thought, Of course I would feel this way, I am just getting over the flu and I had not gotten much sleep the night before. After all, I had just experienced the episode in the store and accepted that I could be diabetic. I put on my jacket and my boots and left the apartment. As I walked through the parking lot to my car, the boots felt very heavy and it was difficult to walk. With each step, an inordinate amount of energy was exerted. I passed it off as a combination of my being tired and the cold and snow affecting my walk up the hill to my car. By the time I got to the car, I was exhausted and felt that I was not going to be able to make it. As I began to drive, something said to me that I should go to the hospital and get checked out. I knew that this was more than the flu and not just a normal bout with being fatigued and I should no longer ignore that my body was going through something and I needed to know what it was. When I arrived at the hospital, the nurse asked me strange questions like had I been drinking any blood, bat juice or taking any weird drugs? I thought the questions were really strange and she seemed especially perplexed by what she was seeing as she proceeded to check me out and ask questions. She left the room and after some time, she returned and advised me that she needed to admit me into the hospital in order to run more tests. This was the Christmas season and I was really busy at work and thought this was a good time to be hospitalized, because I needed the rest. I called my girlfriend and informed her that they were going to admit me and was admitted on December 8, 2008. She came to the hospital and stayed the night with

Jonathan Collins

me. The next morning, I woke up thinking that it was a normal morning. I stretched and made an attempt to get out of the bed and go use the restroom. Attempting to get up revealed that my legs didn't work. Unable to swing my legs out of the bed, led to an overwhelming sense of disbelief and I just thought I needed to get the nurses to come and fix this problem. Shocked but not afraid, I was thinking, "OMG what now…" My immediate agenda was to get to the restroom and rid myself of the urine. At that moment, I realized that we take the small things that we do day to day, for granted. When we need to use the bathroom, we just get up and go. I realized that I could not. I expressed to my girlfriend that I could not move my legs in order to get up and she came over and used my feet to swing my legs to the side of the bed. It was then that I realized I could not stand up on my own.

We looked at each other with a dismissive giggle as she helped me get off the bed and assisted me into the bathroom. When she began to leave, I told her that I needed her to pull my pants down for me. Now this was a little embarrassing, as a man, to have your girlfriend pull your pants down so that you can use the bathroom. Although we were really close, I must admit that this was quite uncomfortable. While sitting on the toilet, I was trying to understand or come up with some logical explanation as to why it was so hard for me to walk. Once I finished, she had to come back and pull my pants up and help me back to the bed. After I got back into the bed, we called the nurse and explained that I could not move my legs or walk for myself. They didn't know what was wrong with me and were quite puzzled. After being in the hospital for a couple of days, I was seen by a neurologist. Once he completed a checkup and reviewed my chart, the neurologist concluded that I had Guillain – Barre Syndrome. The doctors felt like they caught it really early, which is always a good thing. I had never heard of this condition (Gui what syndrome?), but I felt the doctors knew what was best and I was ready to do whatever necessary to get better. Totally underestimating what I had just heard, I did not understand the severity of what had been said. I was thinking they could just give me a prescription for pills that would cure what I was dealing with. I think I may have been in a state of denial. Whenever faced with any type of challenge or adversity, my mantra has always been to do whatever I have to do to fix it and keep it moving. GBS was not an easy fix.

Requesting that I sign authorization for the Doctors to start a procedure called Plasmapheresis, the medical team said it was imperative that we begin right away. They began the procedure and told me that I had to go into surgery immediately. They had to put a catheter in my neck. Before starting the procedure, the nurse told me that they were going to numb my neck. I felt a needle stick me about 10 to 12 times and I remember thinking that wasn't so bad. After the nurse had finished numbing my neck, he began to count down 3, 2, 1 and oh my gosh! The catheter felt as if it was the size of an adult man's finger being shoved into my neck and down my chest. There was so much pressure, I could feel every centimeter as they continued to shove it further and further. This pain was excruciating, and I began screaming loudly. The pain was so intense that the vicious grip I had on the hand of the nurse that was holding my hand resulted in a broken hand. I broke her hand and she was crying right along with me, as we were both in pain. Once they finished the procedure, they gave me pain medicine that forced me into a deep sleep. When I awoke, I just knew that I had been dreaming until I tried to move my neck and realized that I could not move it freely. It was stiff, and the point of incision was very painful. My girlfriend called my family and they all came to visit me. They were baffled, confused and very concerned; wanting to know what was going on with me, what happened to me and why. I put forth every effort to remain calm and not cause them to worry any more than they were already. I was closest to my two younger sisters and I could tell they were very afraid. They were trying their best to hide their fear and emotions so they would not upset me any further and cause me to worry about them.

A few days after my first surgery, I remember asking my cousin to help me to the restroom. Isaac was 6ft 1 and around 265 pounds (compared to my being 6ft 4 and 225 pounds at the time). At this point I was in complete denial! The nurses insisted that I use the bedpan or the urinal instead of trying to get up and go to the restroom. My ego would not allow me to use the bed pan. In my head that was for old folks or people that were disabled. Isaac was very hesitant when asked to assist me to the restroom, but I begged and begged him and eventually convinced him that we could do it together. He helped me to my feet and we literally made it 5 feet away from the bed.

I couldn't walk and was not even able to hold myself up which made it feel as if he was carrying dead weight, and he was unable to assist me. This is when things began to set in for me and my reality that "I CAN'T WALK" became clear. We both realized that we weren't going to make it to the bathroom, and we were too far from the bed for him to carry me back. Isaac felt defeated and I was very apologetic. I didn't want to get him into any trouble for getting me out of the bed without calling the nurse, so I told him to just lie me down on the floor and we would call the nurse together. The story we came up with was that I had fallen out of bed and that's what we stuck with.

View from the Outside

What impacted me the most about Jonathan's experience was when he could not talk, and he could only communicate via eye blinks and head nods. I was in college at the time and my mom had told me about his condition, but I could not imagine how bad it was. It really frightened me to see him in that sort of state. It was a shock that's hard to put into words.

Jonathan has always been a physically active and energetic person, and to see him in a state where he couldn't move was very distressing. At the time, we didn't know if he was going to get better, so the idea that he could be stuck this way for the rest of his life was very scary. I can only imagine how he himself personally handled it.

Emotionally I was very sad, but I tried not to show it and just tried to remain hopeful for him.

What I gained from Jonathan's journey is to always keep your faith in God and the power of prayer. Sometimes in life when things become hard you just have a put your faith in God and trust that he has a plan and that he'll guide you. I also learned the importance of family sticking together. Family can be a source of strength when you are at your weakest. Our family really mobilized and came together in support of Jonathan. Our family bond is really unshakable and I'm extremely thankful for it.

Another thing I gained is the importance of never giving up, and no matter how bad things get, always persevere. Throughout it all he never gave up hope. And I think that is what lead him to get better. He kept fighting and fighting. I think his whole situation served as inspiration to everyone around him. Even the doctors and nursing staff were amazed. What it ultimately taught me is that with faith in God and the strength of family, no challenge is insurmountable.

I think everybody in our family came out of the experience a stronger person. For me, it renewed my faith in God. I saw the miracles he can produce and the importance of being there for others.

Isaac Walker (cousin)

Chapter 3

What is Guillain-Barre Syndrome?

"Your Illness does not define you. Your strength and courage do"
-Unknown

Before I was diagnosed, I had never heard of Guillain-Barre syndrome (GBS) and wanted to share it with others as most don't know what it is. It is a rare autoimmune disorder in which the body's immune system mistakenly attacks the peripheral nerves and damages their myelin insulation. It affects 1 out of 200,000 individuals and is very rare but is very serious. The damage prevents the nerves from transmitting signals to the brain, resulting in the patient becoming weak and suffering with numbness or paralysis. Although the exact causes of Guillain-Barre syndrome are unknown, the Centers for Disease Control and Prevention (CDC) has found that about 66% of patients develop it following a bout of diarrhea or a respiration infection. It can be triggered by an infection, surgery, or vaccination. It is suggested that the immune system may be responding in an improper way to a previous illness, which could cause it to spin out of control. One of the most common risk factors for the syndrome is Campylobacter Jejuni infection, which is generally caused by bacteria in undercooked food.

It has been said by the Mayo Clinic that patients with the syndrome will often notice tingling and weakness in the feet and legs first and then spreads to the upper body and arms. In a few cases, it starts in the upper body first. After the muscle weakness comes difficulty with walking, making facial movements (which can affect eating and speaking) and can even have an adverse effect on breathing.

The symptoms of the syndrome can be divided into three phases:

1. The Progressive phase, which can last anywhere from a few days to 2 weeks
2. The plateau phase, which consists of persistent symptoms and lasts for a few days or weeks.
3. The improvement phase, when recovery takes place, usually lasts six to twelve months, although for some people it could take as long as three years.

About half of patients with GBS complain of severe pain that is experienced with the slightest of movements. The most common sites of pain are the shoulder, girdle, back and posterior thighs.

Because GBS is a syndrome and not a specific disease, there are different forms of it. The main types include **Acute Demyelinating Polyradiculoneuropathy (AIDP),** which is the most common form in the US and is characterized by muscle weakness that starts in the feet and legs and progress upward. Other major forms include **Miller Fisher Syndrome (MFS)** which the Mayo Clinic says begins in the eyes and is associated with an unsteady walk. MFS is most common in Asia; **Acute Motor Axonal Neuropathy (AMAN)** also known as Chinese paralytic syndrome-Anti-GD3 antibodies are found more frequently in A MAN; and finally, **Acute Panautonomic Neuropathy** which is associated with a high mortality rate, owing to cardiovascular involvement, and associated dysrhythmias.

How is GBS diagnosed?

After a medical history and thorough physical examination, the following may then be recommended.

1. Spinal tap which entails withdrawing a small amount of fluid from the spinal canal in your lower back. The fluid is tested for a change that occurs when GBS is present.

2. Electromyography is when thin needle electrodes are inserted into the muscles your doctor wants to study. The electrodes measure nerve activity in the muscles.

3. Nerve conduction studies. Electrodes are taped to the skin above your nerves. A small shock is passed through the nerve to measure the speed of nerve signals.

Although there is no cure for GBS there are two types of treatments that can speed up recovery and reduce the severity of the illness. They are Plasma exchange (Plasmapheresis) and Immunoglobulin therapy. Physical therapy and pain medication are also necessary when treating GBS.

The treatment that they gave me was Plasmapheresis. This is when the liquid portion of your blood (plasma) is removed and separated from your blood cells. Once the blood cells are put back into the body, more plasma is manufactured to make up for what was removed. The goal is to rid the plasma of certain antibodies that contribute to the immune system's attack on the peripheral nerves. This information was obtained from Mayoclinic.com.

Chapter 4

My Guardian Angel

"All God's angels come to us disguised"
-James Russell Lowell

Next I was introduced to an occupational therapist, Kyle. He was assigned to assess my condition. I was still in pain and everything was confusing and very fresh as everyone was still quite uncertain about my condition, thus causing his initial visit to be very frustrating for me. He asked me a lot of questions in an attempt to figure out what I could and could not do. Other questions were being asked in order to get to know me. Kyle and I had a lot in common and as time progressed, we really bonded.

He seemed to become more of my guardian angel than my therapist, always anticipating my next move and calculating all of the possible outcomes; good or bad. He was there for every stage of my hospital visit.I remember one particular day in therapy, he was working with me on how to bathe myself. I was sitting in the shower and he was sitting behind the shower curtain, talking me through it. When I was almost done, he asked me if I had washed my feet. I informed him that I wasn't able to wash my feet because I didn't have full control of my body yet and couldn't bend over that far. He insisted that I try. With great hesitation, I leaned in a little to reach my feet. As you may guess, gravity quickly pulled my body forward and all I could see was that I was about to fall and bang my head on the faucet. Immediately, fear struck me and out of nowhere, Kyle's hand reached through the curtain, grabbed me in my chest and pushed me back up on the seat. He was very calm and collected as if he was expecting that to happen. He just wanted me to at least attempt to wash my feet. After all, I can't continue never washing my feet and always expecting someone else to wash them for me. It all happened so quickly that I was a little baffled as to what happened. Kyle later became very influential in my life. He was very passionate and cared a lot about his job and his patients. I am grateful for his expertise, his care and his concern.

A View from the Outside

I was able to work with Jonathan throughout his hospital stay. This included in the Intensive Care unit, Medical Surgical unit, and Inpatient Rehab as he experienced his decline and then recovery from Guillain-Barre Syndrome. At the time, I was only out of school for Occupational Therapy for a couple years and felt that this was the most important case I have had so far in my career. Only a few years separated us in years and lifestyle. I had the privilege to meet some of Jonathan's family members who were the same age as my parents and grandparents. This made me feel that we had a lot in common. He also shared his passion for playing basketball. I feel that this was a significant driver of determination for his recovery, but I believe also frustrated him because he had so much difficulty doing the most basic movement. I think there were times that he believed he may never play basketball again. I took it upon myself to give him an item that was important to me, a Michael Jordan Bulls poster. My hope was that it would be a reminder that he has an ambitious but achievable goal and inspire him to remain determined and steadfast in the more difficult times.

I first met Jonathan for an initial evaluation in the ICU after he was diagnosed with Guillain Barre Syndrome. I provided some treatment/ activity to help with safe transfers, strengthening activity, and attempt to preserve what function he had at the time. He began receiving medication treatment which the purpose was to mitigate some of the paralysis progression. It became evident that he was not getting significant benefit from this medication treatment, and I observed a progressive decline in strength which ultimately resulted in complete paralysis of his body and facial muscles and he required repeated periods of intubation (tube in his mouth for breathing assistance).

I was one of few people on his care team who worked with him prior to this decline. I developed a connection to Jonathan and felt somewhat responsible and protective of Jonathan because I was able to establish a rapport before this low point phase of his illness. I knew this was recently a healthy, autonomous, thriving young man who continued to be fully aware, alert and oriented, but had no way to express his fear, anxiety, and frustration, let alone his basic needs of being too hot/cold, thirsty, in pain, etc.

No technique of writing, blink, mouthing words, or any other techniques would have allowed successful communication.

As one of his caregivers, I felt quite helpless and this further bolstered my sense of protectiveness throughout his recovery

I think what I gained the most from my experience with Jonathan is that he helped me grow significantly, as a therapist and caregiver, in terms of empathy. He helped me understand how it is quite important that a critical illness impacts a person. That sounds overly simplistic, so let me give an example for Jonathan. He was experiencing several losses during this period of his life and illness. He lost a romantic relationship, friends, a home, the function of his body, and his own autonomy. His emotional expression of these losses was hard for me to understand at first. He was angry at times, withdrawn, resistant to participate, and had a hard time celebrating success/progress. But the framework of "stages of grief "gave me some insight. He and others I have worked with exhibit denial, anger, bargaining, depression, and hopefully, eventually acceptance. I observed Jonathan go through each of these stages on and off throughout his time at the hospital. I did the best I could with the knowledge and experience I had at the time, but he taught me quite a bit about how I can acknowledge this important aspect of a person's experience with disability. I have used this knowledge with much of my patient interaction throughout my career.

Kyle, Occupational Therapist

One of the nurses shared with me that there were two other people in the hospital with GBS. They were much older than me and seemed to be doing well. Meanwhile, my respiratory system was getting weaker and weaker. I had to go through nine Plasmapheresis procedures which entailed hooking me up to a dialysis machine for an hour to an hour and a half. Imagine being hot and cold at the same time and feeling as though someone was reaching into your body and pulling out your soul. I started having spasms and anxiety attacks while going through the procedure. These spasms became rather intrusive to my daily existence. They would come on suddenly for no apparent reason. One day, my son's mother brought my 18- month old son to the hospital to see me and I began to have spasms.

I remember thinking that I was going to die in front of my son. He had to be removed from my room until the spasms ceased. My family, my church family and neighborhood friends were also there visiting me. My church family would pray with me and read the bible to me often. I can definitely say that I had a lot of support and prayers going up for me during this time of sickness and uncertainty.

My father came to stay a week with me. This meant a lot to me because my father was like my idol and was my only living parent. He was always someone that was really strong and never showed weakness and pain. I must admit that it was hard to be tough while lying in the hospital bed in pain and almost paralyzed. I was doing my very best to be strong and not have him see me weak. For this reason, I tried to mask any emotions. I remember one particular day, my dad was in my hospital room talking to one of my friends, when I began having a spasm. My dad had his back to me, and my friend was facing me, but they were talking intensely at the time and did not notice. I felt like I was about to die and refused to say anything to him. It was the longest, most difficult spasm I believe I ever had. My body had locked up. My friend finally looked at me just as it was ending. He gasped and pointed at me fearfully and my dad turned around and grabbed my hand until it was over. Although the spasm was awful, this was definitely a special moment for me. Meanwhile, my lung capacity was getting weaker and weaker. I could speak only at a slight whisper. It was difficult to turn my head, move my eyes and facial muscles.

I eventually found out that the other two people that were in the hospital at the same time as me with GBS had passed away. This was disheartening. As I began to get worse and worse, I accepted that I might die, and I began to prepare for death. I gave away money to my sisters and started giving them advice about life and men. I wanted them to be secure when I left them.

One day my lungs actually collapsed. I was on a lot of medication that caused me to hallucinate. My cousin, Jasmine, was in the room with me and I remember asking my nurse to push my two beds together so that I wouldn't fall between them. I was actually lying on one bed hallucinating. She kept fluffing the pillows behind me and I remember telling her that the pillows being fluffed was not helping.

I was using every ounce of strength to speak to her and I got frustrated because she would not do what I needed her to do, which was push the two beds (that only existed in my head) together. With all the strength I could muster up, I began to scream using my last breath. She ran from the room and came back with flashing red lights and a man that was trying to cover my face and kill me, so I thought. In all actuality, he was trying to put the oxygen mask over my face in order to help me breathe. This was an absolute emergency and it felt as though all of the white coats and blue flashing lights were surrounding me on my bed. I blacked out for an undetermined amount of time. I awoke to both of my hands bound to the hospital bed. I was terrified because I couldn't speak, couldn't hear and was wondering why my hands were bound to the bed. I looked up and saw my family standing around me crying. I was having an out of body experience and felt that I was dead. I was really dead. I didn't know what was real and what was not. I blacked out again. When I woke up the 2nd time, a nurse explained that my lungs had collapsed, and I had a respirator in my throat pumping oxygen into my lungs. There were tubes, wires and machines all over my body. I spent about 10 days in the hospital like this. My family was in and out and as I finally began to get a little more strength in my hands and wrists, they used paper, pencil and letters to communicate with me. It was explained to me that if my lungs did not get better soon, they would have to remove the respirator and place a permanent trachea tube in my throat. If the respirator remained too long, it could set up a bacterial infection and this needed to be avoided. Prayer warriors from my church began to come in daily and pray with me.

On Dec. 24th the nurse explained that my lungs were showing small improvement and she would attempt to remove the respirator from my throat. When she prepared to remove the respirator, I was so excited and overjoyed that I would finally be able to hear my voice again. I pondered the first word I wanted to hear myself say. I recalled my uncle telling me once that when you could say nothing else, just call on the name of Jesus. When the nurse removed the respirator, I gasped so loud and hard due to all of the phlegm that had accumulated in my throat. It was as if I had vomited all over myself. I yelled as loud as I could "Jesus!" The nurse looked at me in amazement as if to say "wow!" This was actually Christmas Day. I thought, what a wonderful Christmas gift for me! I later went through my 9th and final Plasmapheresis. I was grateful that these treatments were done. I had dropped from 235Ibs to 140Ibs.

Chapter 5
No Goodbye

"Perspectives are like batteries. You can see the positive or the negative, and they'll keep you charged up, if you replace them often enough."
- Curtis Tyrone Jones

January 1, 2009, I was transported to the rehab unit. At this time, I was completely paralyzed and needed no more medical attention. The catheter in my neck, the catheter in my bladder, along with the G tube that was used to feed me, had all been removed. The only tube remaining was in the side of my neck which was used to administer any necessary mediation and run tests. I was so excited because I could literally feel the progress of me getting one step closer to leaving the hospital. I noticed my girlfriend was acting a little different towards me. The night before, which was New Year's Eve, I had asked her to stay with me and watch the ball drop. She declined and said that she was tired and had a lot to do the next day. I watched the ball drop on TV with one of my nurses. It was a very emotional moment for me as I had always been with friends, family and loved ones on New Year's Eve. I later found out from a friend that she had attended the same New Year's Eve party that he attended. I didn't want to believe it but deep down in my heart I knew what he was saying was true. It was so painful to hear the truth; it literally started eating away at my spirit.

After some time, I was told that I could begin eating regular foods but would be on a special diet that consisted of pureed foods. I was so excited because I loved food and had not eaten any food since early December and was oblivious as to what pureed foods consisted of. When they brought the food, it was covered and smelled so good. When the nutritionist uncovered my food, I saw a pile of yellow (mac and cheese), a pile of green (green beans) and the only thing that was recognizable, which was the pile of apple sauce. I was so lost, it felt like each time I took two steps forward, something happened to knock me back five steps. I cried out to God asking, "What did I do to deserve this, I just want to eat regular food!" I could not feed myself, and this made the food even less enjoyable. My two sisters along with my girlfriend assisted with feeding me. Trying to eat was very frustrating because I could not close my mouth or assist with eating the food. It was similar to feeding an infant child. All I could do was lick and swallow. The muscles in my face had not recovered 100% yet.

This turned into a disastrous ordeal for both me and the person trying to feed me. Most of the food ended up running down my chin and onto my clothing. I know this was not just hard on me, but it was hard on my family who just wanted to help. I was frustrated because I was hungry and could not eat like a normal person and because they not just had to see me like this but feed me as well. I noticed that my girlfriend began to come visit less and less, until finally one day she never came back. Without a call, a text, an email and no explanation the person that I had loved dearly and shared my time and experiences with for the past several years just walked out of my life. I did not understand at the time, but I realize that everyone is not equipped to be what you need in your life during the difficult times. People are in our lives for seasons, reasons and very few for a lifetime. My sudden sickness was tough on me and it was definitely tough on her as neither of us understood it. I was paralyzed and couldn't even feed myself. I had no choice but to be present to go through what I was going through; however, she didn't have to stay, and she chose not to.

I became more and more depressed. I wanted to be optimistic, but I had lost so much; my ability to walk, play basketball, feed myself, my independence, my job and now my girlfriend. The nurses would hear me crying in my room night after night and they called in a psychologist to speak with me. I was not in the proper state of mind to receive from him at that time. Anger and frustration always took over when he came into my room and I would ask him why he was there and tell him that there was nothing wrong and I did not need his assistance. I was not crazy, I was paralyzed. The truth was that I was depressed and emotionally distraught and he was just not the right one to help. He failed to talk to me and get to know me and what I was going through before asking me to tell him how I felt. Maybe if it had been someone closer to my age, who looked more like me, it would have been more impactful and maybe not. I was in a dark place and had no idea what would help me, other than rewinding the time and events back to before I became ill.

My medical team consisted of a physical therapist, an occupational therapist and a speech therapist. My physical therapist was more like a personal trainer and I didn't like her because she challenged me to do things that I felt I could not do. She massaged my legs often as if she was trying to make them work properly. It felt as if she tried every trick in the book she knew or had learned to help me recover and become physically stronger again. After each session, I had to wait in a room in a wheelchair for my transporter to come and pick me up to transport me back to my room. I felt so defeated and I didn't have an "I can do it mentality" but rather felt that I could not do anything. I was in the physical therapy area with older people that completed physical therapy. They suffered from knee replacements, strokes, hip replacements and even brain surgery and I would sit and wave good-bye as they left the hospital, walking and smiling. This was more depressing as I sat there unable to move, waiting for someone to come and wheel me back to my room and put me back into my bed.

I was still having so much trouble eating that I became completely discouraged and I refused to eat. The medical team threatened to put the G Tube back in my neck if I didn't start eating. They eventually switched me from drinking two ensures per day to a carnation breakfast drink which had more calories. At this point, I had dropped down to 140 pounds.

I began going on weekly outings in order to get me accustomed to going out in public in my condition. My therapist took me to restaurants and other places that I would have to frequent using a wheelchair. They were essentially preparing me to live in the world outside of the hospital as a normal person with paralysis.

The haunting truth was that I was terrified of leaving the hospital and living on my own.

Having become comfortable with my nurses and therapists assisting me, I didn't want to even attempt to envision how my life would be on the outside of the hospital. Fear and depression had become my constant companions. The myriad of questions invaded my mind repeatedly concerning leaving the hospital. Who will assist me day to day (I can't put this pressure on my family)? How will I get where I need to go? How will I take care of myself at home? What happens if I fall? Will all the places I frequent have wheelchair access? What will my life look like from the wheelchair? Who will love me now? And many more. Each time my being released was mentioned, the constant fear that I felt was intensified.

A View from the Outside

Although I knew Jonathan before he was diagnosed with Guillain-Barre Syndrome, my presence in his life manifested more as he was just learning to walk, without assistance. I can remember having a conversation with him, after we left church. We sat in the car and I listened to him explain how he wanted to turn this experience into motivation for others who are going through similar situations. He talked about finding his purpose in life, and how he wanted to live a more meaningful life that also involved a deeper relationship with God, his family, his son and developing his own family with a wife and children. This was so impactful for me because that wasn't the same Jonathan I knew before Guillain-Barre Syndrome.

It was such an inspiration just to see him in a different light.

Although I saw him as motivated, I couldn't help but feel sympathy for him every time I saw him. He walked with a slight limp and struggled to walk up a flight of stairs. However, witnessing the "new" Jonathan (from the way he carried himself, his conversation, to his demeanor) was inspiring and becoming.

Jonathan's experience caused me to look at my own life differently and make some changes. Changes that included my relationship with God, family and friends. In a way I was able to gain a new perspective on life, knowing that things can be worse. Meanwhile, discovering what I believe God gifted me as my purpose in life.

Marquia Gatlin (daughter's mother)

Chapter 6
Acceptance

"If there's life, there is hope."
-Stephen Hawking

"Mr. Collins, you must accept the fact that there is a 99% possibility that you may never walk again!" said the Doctor. My friend Josh was in the hospital room with me at the time. I am so grateful that Josh was there because, by the time the Dr. left the room, I had already accepted what was spoken over me as my truth. I was sinking down into the ditch of despair and just knew I was not going to walk again. Josh looked at me and said, "Man you are not going to be paralyzed the rest of your life. Don't listen to her, you are going to play basketball again, we are going to hoop." He skipped right over walking and said I would be playing basketball. He not only spoke the words, but he appealed to my passion which was playing basketball. He emphatically told me not to accept what the Dr. said as my truth and he would not allow me to believe anything other than the fact that I would walk again. The reality was that had he not been there, things could have gone a different way for me. When dealing with matters of life and death, we must react quickly.

"Death and life are in the power of the tongue, and those who love it will eat its fruits."

-Proverbs 18:21-23

I said you're right with my mouth, but I was still not completely convinced that I would walk again. I desperately wanted to believe Josh, but the reality of what I was living at the time was more powerful than my faith and my mindset. This was a major lesson for me. It was a huge reminder that our words have power and that we must be mindful of not just what we say, but how we allow ourselves to think. Our mindset shapes what we think, speak and even do. We also have to be careful what we allow others speak over us. Everyone needs a friend like Josh. Someone who will speak up for us and who is not afraid to check us and/or challenge us. When young, we tend to become friends with our neighbors or those that we go to school with or the children of our parent's friends. As we get older, it is important to choose our friends more carefully. It is always necessary to be careful who we have in our circles and call our friends. We can't control our environment, but we can certainly control who we allow into our immediate circle and who we allow to speak into our lives.

I would never have entertained the idea that I could possibly walk again. It took a friend to speak into my life. There are some who would have encouraged me to be realistic and not get my hopes up that I would walk again. I believe in some way that was just what the doctor was doing. She did not want to give me false hope and was encouraging me to learn to live without the full use of my arms and legs, just in case. Doctors operate off their limited medical knowledge and from a medical standpoint it didn't appear that I would make a full recovery. They are trained to teach their patients to accept the unfavorable at times and prepare them for the worse scenario, rather than give them false hope and have the patient feeling that the doctor told them wrong. If they recover, great; but if not, at least they are prepared to live accordingly. I wanted to believe that I could walk again but my reality was overshadowing my beliefs. Again, this is why we need people around us who will be strong and believe, when we are not able to believe for ourselves. Any negativity would have been the wrong thing for me during my journey.

Chapter 7

Suicide Attempt

"You have to be at your strongest when you're
feeling at your weakest."
-Kushandwizdom

My day-to-day became quite monotonous, uneventful and painful. I couldn't see any progress in my condition, but rather all I could see was that I was paralyzed and could not do for myself. Each day I would wake up, have breakfast, take medications, receive a sponge bath, go to occupational therapy, come back, have lunch (pureed foods with ensure or a carnation drink) and then go to physical therapy. Dark moments were constant companions during my time of sickness. I was trying to hold onto the faith that I would get better and the belief that no matter what, God was with me and he had a plan for my healing. After a while, I no longer had the will to live. I felt that I was not living and had not been allowed to die and decided to take matters into my own hands and end it all. I had begun recovering some of my upper body strength and was able to use my arms to assist minimally in my movement. The normal routine was that two nurses would help me out of bed and into my wheelchair in order to transport me to therapy. This particular day, there was only one nurse there to assist me and I had decided to make my move. I thought if I hit my head on the steel bar on the side of the hospital bed just right, surely it would be all over. Right…about…NOW…I calculated as I let go of my grip and withheld any of the assistance that I was giving the nurse; managing to hit my head on the cold, hard steel railing. The tears began to flow profusely as I realized

I was still alive. The nurse, thinking that my hands had slipped, panicked and yelled, "Mr. Collins, are you okay?" Physically, I felt the pain of hitting my head, however the tears were brought on by the emotional pain of knowing that my attempt to end it was unsuccessful. I had not considered the fact that I could have made my bad situation a lot worse. With this futile attempt to take matters into my own hands, I had caused myself more physical and emotional pain, unnecessarily! The lesson in this is that you cannot leave until it is your time. When there is a purpose for your life, you must stay around to fulfill that purpose. Although I was hurting, depressed and afraid, it was not time for me to leave this earth. I had to sit in those feelings and complete my journey. Just think, if my suicide attempt had been successful. My children would not have their father, my family would not have me, and this book would not have been written.

"Nobody will protect you from your suffering. You can't cry it away or eat it away or punch it away. It's just there, and you have to survive it. You have to endure it. And you have to live through it and love it and move on and be better for it and run as far as you can in the direction of your best and happiest dreams across the bridge that was built by your own desire to heal."
-Cheryl Strayed

After the attempt, I began to wonder if I could sell my soul to the devil and if I did, would he allow me to walk the next day? I was sitting in the room with the lights off, staring at my legs and willing them to move, and of course they would not. I was so upset, desperate and emotional and was willing to entertain the devil.

I was overwhelmed with anger, sadness, frustration and the feeling that God was not helping me. Where was He and why was He allowing me to suffer this way? Didn't he love me? The devil is always ready to step in and give us false hope while plotting to kill, steal and destroy us. After some pondering and going back and forth with darkness, the light won. I knew that the devil didn't have the authority or power to give me what I so desperately needed and wanted.

I cried out to God, "PLEASE LORD HELP ME, I'M YOURS! I'LL DO WHATEVER YOU NEED ME TO DO WHENEVER YOU WANT ME TO DO IT. I JUST WANT TO WALK AGAIN!" A day or two later, I had a dream that I had to use the restroom. In the dream, I sat up on the side of the bed and stood up making my way to the restroom. Halfway there, I stopped and looked at my hands and then took a look at my legs and feet and thought what's going on, this can't be real because I can't walk. I instantly woke up from the dream and looked down to find one of my legs was elevated off the bed. This was a very emotional moment for me, I couldn't believe it. It felt as if God heard me pleading for his help and gave me exactly what I needed. Although my leg was only 2.5 inches off the bed, this gave me a glimpse of hope and was a pivotal point in my life. I said to myself, "I AM WALKING OUT OF HERE!" I finally gave in to FAITH!!

I made the choice to believe and live. This was the first step to my actual recovering and overcoming. I began to work really hard, with the therapist and without. I began to push my body and mind to the limit. I had envisioned myself walking and that was now my end goal. If you can see it, you can do it. I had begun to manifest my goal. The dream was so vivid, it certainly shifted my whole mindset. It was short but it was very profound. This was a turning point for me as I no longer allowed depression and fear to drive me but began allowing faith along with anger, frustration and determination to drive me. This is a prime example of why we need faith. We can allow fear to hold us back completely or we can exercise our faith and believe, and it will propel us forward. When you are in a tough place, whether it is physical, spiritual, emotional or financial, if you can muster up the faith to believe, envision yourself in a much better situation and then put in the work, you can make the necessary changes for the better.

Post dream. Determined to walk, I began
exercising and pushing myself hard.

A View from the Outside

It was scary; I had never heard of anything like this before. I knew of a guy in the Army that said he had an auto-immune disease and he said his body shut down. But you think this " happens to other people ".

I believe in God and the power of prayer and in prayers of power. I am convinced that God showed favor on Jonathan. I was worried that this situation might cost him his life . But when you look at him through a wide lens, God was at work even then.

My nephew went to the ER thinking he had the flu; that was a minor miracle because most of the time a person just gets medicine over the counter. God placed the right doctor in the ER who recognized that was not the flu and admitted him .

I had a medical scare in 2016-2017 and I did not know how things would turn out. I feel on a subconscious level that I tried to stand strong like my nephew. Our family is close knit and I feel our combined prayers and our love and support helped him survive.

Uncle Ben Walker

Chapter 8
The Will to Overcome

*"Although the world is full of suffering, it is
also full of the overcoming of it."*
-Helen Keller

While thinking back over my journey, I
had the epiphany that this major experience
had changed the trajectory of my life. I had
been afflicted and deeply hurt, but I had also
overcome and am a better man and father
because of it. During this difficult time in my
life, I definitely felt like I could not escape the
vicissitudes of life and had to adapt to the
changes they brought. I had to overcome on 3
levels: Emotionally, Spiritually and Physically.

It was most difficult for me to heal emotionally.
According to Webster's dictionary, emotion is a
natural instinctive state of mind deriving from

one's circumstances, mood or relationships with others. I didn't know it then, because of the mountain of pain and the valley of troubles and defeat I was experiencing , but I now know that it was all a part of my journey. I fell deeper into depression when my girlfriend left me, stepmom that raised me for ten years never came to visit me at all during the four months I was in the hospital and friends that I considered brothers never even called while I was in the hospital. I never considered that I would have to go through the worst ordeal that I had ever experienced in my life. It was not their journey and I could not expect any of them to make my journey with me, as they had their own. What a lesson to learn during such a painful time in my life. We often get so caught up and inundated with those that we love, that we completely lose ourselves.

I realized that I loved my girlfriend too much. This started to wake me up Spiritually. I had put everything else, including my girlfriend, ahead of God and this caused a great deal of emotional stress for me. I had to fight to arrest my emotions, not allow them to control me and learn to love myself.

"The scars you can't see are the hardest to heal."

Spiritually, I had to walk it out with God, and I am still a work in progress as our spiritual growth must be cultivated daily. I know I have a real relationship with God, and I feel like I now know who he is, and I respect the power he has. I always knew he was real, however going through all that I went through, was confirmation that he is real. It taught me that no one or nothing is to be put before Him.

Forced to sit in the space that I was in until it was over, I saw that all I was going through was necessary for me to get what I needed from the situation. Still somewhat unsure of what was going on but knowing I had done nothing to cause the illness to come upon me; I could do nothing to make it stop and I could only deal with the hand that I had been dealt. There were many moments where I thought God was non-existent in my life. These moments were accompanied with anger towards HIM because I felt like he was not helping me, and I could not understand why he had allowed me to become sick with such a vicious illness. What did I do that was so wrong? Was I being punished for something? Will I die from this?

Those were only a few of the looming questions. It was much later that the clarity flooded in and I was able to see that my journey was used to help me and many others.

Those on the outside looking in were able to see my physical progression and could see the physical obstacles that I overcame. I had gone from being in ICU for the whole month of December to being in rehab January, February and March. I had gone from tubes coming out of my body at several different entries, not being able to open my mouth, chew my food, feed myself, use my arms nor legs to completely functioning on my own. There was a time during my process that I was so fearful because I felt that no one understood what I was feeling or going through.

Some days I was smiling but behind the scenes there was much pain and each day was a series of daunting tasks. It was extremely difficult not being able to communicate with anyone. During one of the most difficult times, it was as if I was encased by a full body cast with two holes for eyes and two holes for ears. I could see and hear but had absolutely no way of communicating my needs, my wants, my fears or my pain. It is a misconception that people have that paralysis only affects arms and legs, as they tend to forget facial muscles and motor skills. Blinking my eyes or using my mouth to form words or even chew proved to be impossible.

I had therapy to retrain me on these simple tasks. I knew fighting to recover physically was a must. I had so much to prove. At one point it felt like it was impossible, but once I was convinced I could do it, there was no turning back. Rage fueled me. Proving people wrong fueled me. Not receiving help from the government fueled me. Most of all, my Faith began to fuel me. It is amazing what we can do when we make a choice and put some action behind it. I chose to live, and I chose to believe and put the hard work with that belief.

First day home from the hospital. Down under 150 pounds.

Chapter 9

For My Good

"It was good for me to be afflicted so that I might learn your decrees"
-Psalm 119:71 NIV version

As a result of my journey, the spiritual growth was unfathomable for me, my family and friends. It was expressed to me by many who saw me suffering from Guillain-Barre Syndrome that it was difficult watching me go through the process. They also expressed that once I completed the journey, their faith in God was stronger and they believe in his mercy and power and know that he is a healer. If one is never sick, they don't know what it means to be healed. I never knew how strong I was until I was put in a position to be strong. I had to believe in myself and know that I would walk again before it could happen. I visualized myself walking and then became obsessed over it. I had to physically push myself, but it first began in my mind. If you have dreams that you want to accomplish and obstacles you need to overcome, you must first believe that you can accomplish them and be willing to put in the hard work. Be prepared to face your fears and the obstacles that will arise. It will not be easy but anything that is worth having rarely ever comes easily. As a result of my journey, I am a better man, father, friend and person. I am wiser and stronger.

While in the hospital, I felt that I was missing out on the whole world and was ready to get back to life. Even then, I was putting everything before God. I was rushing back to basketball, my relationships, my job, money and my friends. Actually, I should having been running to God, trying to get closer to him because he is my source. None of those things, I thought I was missing out on, were more important than my health or my relationship with Him. The money had no value and the relationships were empty. The truth is, nothing I wanted was even possible without God. I felt I had been stripped of everything. Even while lying flat on my back with no use of my legs, I still did not get it. It was not until I had the spiritual encounter with God after trying to sell my soul to the devil, that I really got it. I finally completely surrendered to God and said, "Ok, whatever you want, I surrender, I give up!" My willingness to give up and surrender in that moment automatically gave me access to greater wisdom, strength and ultimately made me better.

I had to face the fact that "I was chosen for this". I had to walk through and live out my journey to get to a point where I was rooted and grounded in God. I had to go through the process in order to help others see. I was used to show others the power of healing. My family and friends were able to go through parts of it with me and see how important faith is. My pain and suffering was my test and I had to endure it, embrace it, keep pushing through to the end of it and learn from it as it ultimately brought me to the place where I now have a testimony to share with others; not something I heard or something I read but something I have experienced. I have been given a new understanding of the saying that I don't look like what I have been through; a new understanding of being in the fire and not getting burned; being under water and not drowning. Looking at me today, you would never know that I went through all that I went through! I SURVIVED Guillain-Barre Syndrome and I SURVIVED my suicide attempt. I am a SURVIVOR!

I know that I was chosen for this. God knew that I was strong enough to handle it, long before I knew it and he chose to use me to help others. In your darkest hour please know that you are not alone and that you can weather any storm that you are faced with if you only believe you can. Never give up on the process and know that you have everything you need already inside you! Just tap into it and strengthen your inner man. Stay Positive and keep negative people out of your ear and out of your circle. Find that scripture, that story, that quote, that song that gives you hope in between prayers and people. Another important point to remember is that IT IS NOT ABOUT YOU! There are some things that we suffer for others and not for ourselves. Sometimes we are used to show others that they can. Sometimes we go through to show others that they can make it through. While on this journey called life, we will all fall at some point. We will go through things that really get us down, make us cry and maybe even cause us to feel some depression and self-pity, but we cannot stay there and wallow in that pain. Take a much-needed moment and get it all out. Then, we must get up quickly, dust ourselves off, center ourselves and continue on in the journey; we have no time to waste. When I was at my lowest point, my sister found an old iPod that I had lost and brought it to me in the hospital. On that iPod, was a song by Marvin Sapp entitled

"Never Would Have Made It". I played this song repeatedly during my hospital stay and it gave me strength to keep going. This song is still dear to my heart as I know that I never would have made it without God. Now I can actually see how he was there for me and how he never left me. Keep fighting and never give up! I can honestly say that because of God's mercy, my faith, hard work and perseverance through what I thought was the worst thing I have ever had to experience, I'm stronger, I'm wiser, I'm better!

Jonathan Collins

*"The relation between parents and children
is essentially based on teaching."*

-Gilbert Highet

My kids have always been my inspiration to do bigger and better things. I grew up with strong father figures in my life that provided me with a great example. I am so grateful that I Survived, I am alive, and I am able to sow into the lives of my kids. They were not there to witness my struggle through GBS, however I do want them to learn something valuable from my struggle; Never give up, trust in God and have Faith while putting your hard work with it. Realizing that I can't watch over and protect them at every second, it's always been my goal to teach them how to get up once life knocks them down. Knowing that kids always repeat your actions more than what you ask of them, it is important that

I do my best to always stand up stronger,

wiser and better.

"Life is like riding a bicycle. To keep your balance, you must keep moving."

-Albert Einstein

*Don't be discouraged. It's often the last key
in the bunch that opens the lock."*

-Author Unknown

*"A winner is someone who gets up one more
time than he is knocked down"*

-Author Unknown

Jonathan Collins

I'm Stronger I'm Wiser I'm Better

Jonathan Collins

Made in USA - North Chelmsford, MA
1112734_9780997780468
05.21.2020 0449